D1606616

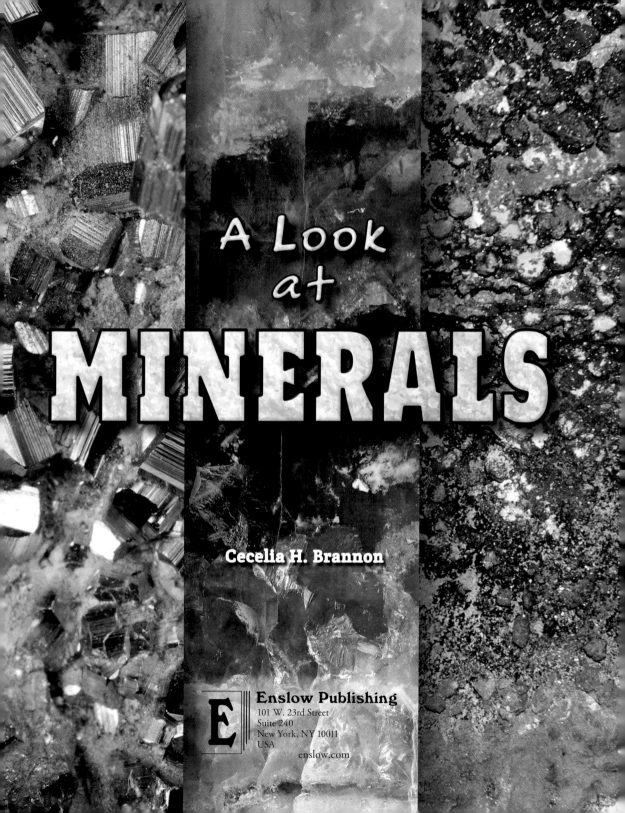

A Look at
at
MINERALS

Cecelia H. Brannon

E | **Enslow Publishing**
101 W. 23rd Street
Suite 240
New York, NY 10011
USA

enslow.com

Published in 2016 by Enslow Publishing, LLC
101 W. 23rd Street, Suite 240, New York, NY 10011

Library of Congress Cataloging-in-Publication Data

Brannon, Cecelia H., author.
  A look at minerals / Cecelia H. Brannon.
    pages cm. — (The rock cycle)
  Audience: Ages 8+
  Audience: Grades 4 to 6.
  ISBN 978-0-7660-7309-8 (library binding)
  ISBN 978-0-7660-7307-4 (pbk.)
  ISBN 978-0-7660-7308-1 (6-pack)
  1. Minerals—Juvenile literature. 2. Geochemical cycles—Juvenile literature. I. Title.
  QE365.2.B73 2016
  549—dc23

                                2015029180

Printed in the United States of America

To Our Readers: We have done our best to make sure all websites in this book were active and appropriate when we went to press. However, the author and the publisher have no control over and assume no liability for the material available on those websites or any websites they may link to. Any comments or suggestions can be sent by e-mail to customerservice@enslow.com.

Photo Credits: Throughout book: Jiri Vaclavek/Shutterstock.com (colorful glittery mineral), Audrius Merfeldas/Shutterstock.com (white salt crystal), patrice6000/Shutterstock.com (tan and white marble); assistant/Shutterstock.com (colorful metallic mineral), Christine Yarusi (series logo, four-rock dingbat); cover, p. 1 Photographee.eu/Shutterstock.com (gold pyrite, left), Nastya Pirieva/Shutterstock.com (fluorite, center), Lucian Milasan/Shutterstock.com (blue mineral, right); p. 4 Juhku/Shutterstock.com; p. 6 Olga Miltsova/Shutterstock.com (top), Peter Hermes Furian/Shutterstock.com (bottom); p. 7 Mopic/Shutterstock.com; p. 8 Zbynek Burival/Shutterstock.com; p. 9 ZeWrestler/Wikimedia Commons/Rockcycle2.jpg/public domain; p. 11 © iStockphoto.com/mykeyruna (top), gab90/Shutterstock.com (bottom); p. 12 Matej Hudovernik/Shutterstock.com; p. 13 snapgalleria/Shutterstock.com; p. 14 © iStockphoto.com/mikeuk; p. 15 Imfoto/Shutterstock.com (top), MarcelClemens/Shutterstock.com (bottom); p. 17 Kevinr4/Shutterstock.com (talc), www.sandatlas.org/Shutterstock.com (gypsum), RATCHANAT BUA-NGERN/Shutterstock.com (calcite), Albert Russ/Shutterstock.com (fluorite, topaz), Imfoto/Shutterstock.com (apatite), Alexandar Iotzov/Shutterstock.com (orthoclase), Fribus Mara/Shutterstock.com (quartz), Karol Kozlowski/Shutterstock.com (corundum), www.royaltystockphoto.com/Shutterstock.com (diamond); p. 18 Anneka/Shutterstock.com; p. 19 Joel Arem/Science Source/Getty Images; p. 20 Jane Rix/Shutterstock.com; p. 21 Albert Russ/Shutterstock.com; p. 22 MarcelClemens/Shutterstock.com; p. 23 Triff/Shutterstock.com; p. 25 Asaf Eliason/Shutterstock.com (top), YolLusZam1802/Shutterstock.com (bottom); p. 26 © iStockphoto.com/Stendec; p. 27 assistant/Shutterstock.com (top), Harry Taylor/Dorling Kindersley/Getty Images (bottom); p. 28 Mark Higgins/Shutterstock.com (top), jps/Shutterstock.com (bottom); p. 29 hxdbzxy/Shutterstock.com.

Contents

These are limestone formations in Gunung Mulu National Park in Borneo. Limestone is made of the mineral calcite.

What Is a MINERAL?

Minerals are natural, inorganic, solid substances that make up rocks. Minerals are made from naturally occurring elements, such as oxygen, calcium, and iron.

Elements are the simplest substance that can exist. A specific mineral is always made up of the same elements no matter what kind of rock it forms.

Some rocks, like limestone, are made of only one mineral. Other rocks have more minerals. This is because heat or pressure forced many different minerals together to create the rock. Most rocks have between two and ten minerals.

Minerals come in many shapes and colors. The elements in them create different looks.

Did You Know?

White quartz has been used throughout history to make jewelry, stone carvings, and tools. Roman naturalist Pliny the Elder (23 AD–79 AD) believed quartz was ice that had been permanently frozen after centuries on earth.

Because minerals form all rocks, they are an important part of the rock cycle. The rock cycle is the process by which rocks are broken down to create new rocks. This cycle has been shaping and reshaping Earth's surface for millions of years.

What Is a **MINERAL?**

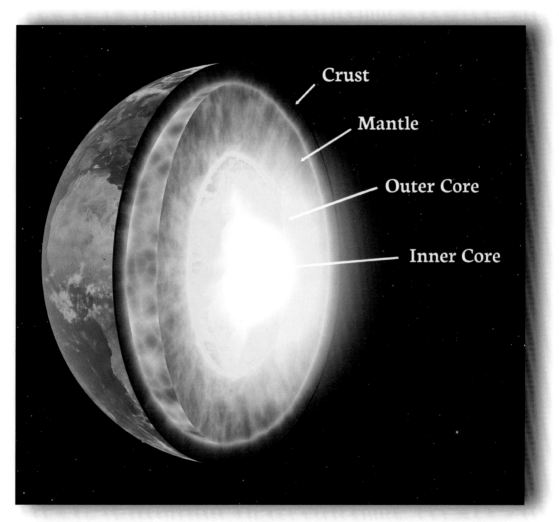

Crust

Mantle

Outer Core

Inner Core

Earth is made of several different layers. The top layer, where we live, is called the crust. Beneath that is the mantle, which is made of liquid magma. The outer core is liquid metal, while the inner core is a solid metal ball.

The rock cycle starts when hot magma rises from the mantle to the crust. Once on the surface, it cools and hardens into igneous rocks. Igneous rocks have minerals in the form of tiny crystals. Over time, these rocks and their minerals are worn down to form sedimentary rocks. Another type of rock, metamorphic rock, is formed when heat and pressure change the minerals inside igneous and sedimentary rocks.

Feldspar is the most common mineral found in Earth's crust.

Sometimes heat and pressure force these minerals together. Other times, the heat and pressure add elements to the minerals, which forms new rocks. This makes minerals an important part of the rock cycle.

What Is a MINERAL?

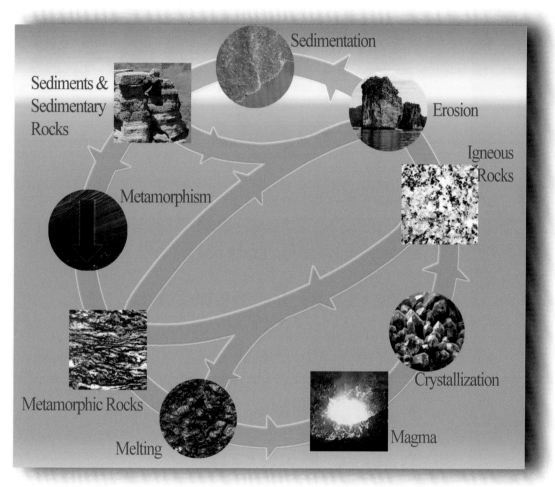

Sedimentation

Sediments &
Sedimentary
Rocks

Erosion

Igneous
Rocks

Metamorphism

Crystallization

Metamorphic Rocks

Magma

Melting

This diagram illustrates how the rock cycle works.
Minerals are included in every step of the rock cycle
because they create each type of rock.

What Are MINERALS Made Of?

Elements are the substances that make up minerals. Some elements include oxygen, hydrogen, sodium, and even gold.

Chemical Composition

In minerals, chemical elements such as oxygen are arranged in a certain way. That arrangement is the mineral's chemical composition. Every mineral has a different chemical composition.

Native Minerals and Compounds

Minerals made of just one element are called native minerals. Some native minerals are made from the elements gold, silver, copper, or mercury.

What Are **MINERALS** Made Of?

Rose quartz, like other quartzes, is made from silicon and oxygen. Rose quartz gets its pink hue from traces of titanium, iron, or manganese.

Native copper has been used for jewelry throughout history. Its more common uses today include plumbing, electrical, and even sculptures like the Statue of Liberty.

Most minerals are combinations of two or more elements. These minerals are called compounds. Salt is made from two chemical elements, sodium and chlorine.

Did You Know?

It is the sodium in the salt water of New York Harbor that has turned Lady Liberty green. This is a natural reaction when copper meets salt, another mineral.

What Are **MINERALS** Made Of?

Atoms and Crystals

Elements are made of tiny substances called atoms. Atoms are the smallest part of an element. An atom is made up of a nucleus and electrons, which are negatively charged particles that move around the nucleus to give the atom energy. Inside the nucleus are protons, which are positively charged particles, and neutrons, which do not have a charge at all.

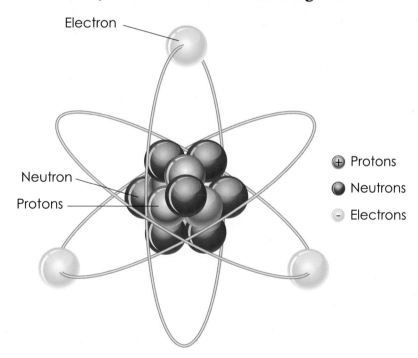

An atom is the building block of everything on Earth. Solids, liquids, gasses, and plasma are all made of atoms.

The atoms in a mineral are always arranged in a particular pattern. Atoms are able to arrange themselves in these various patterns through a tiny electrical charge they give off. This charge causes some of the atoms to stick together. The atoms that stick together in a mineral are called crystals.

Scientists called geologists study the crystals' patterns to figure out what kind of mineral they are looking at.

What Are **MINERALS** Made Of?

Crystals come in many different shapes. The mineral halite has crystals that are shaped like cubes. The mineral zircon has crystals that are shaped like two pyramids stuck together. Crystals can also have smooth, flat sides, called faces. If you broke a mineral into tiny pieces, every crystal inside each piece would have the same pattern.

Zircon is a mineral found in zirconium, which is one of the strongest compounds on Earth.

Did You Know?

Did you know that you eat minerals every day? The mineral known as halite is more commonly called salt!

How to Identify a MINERAL

A harder mineral will always scratch a softer mineral. Scientists test hardness by scratching one mineral with another and comparing the results to a chart called the Mohs' scale. The scale goes from 1 to 10. The mineral that is listed as number 1 is the softest mineral—talc. It is so soft you can scratch it with your fingernail. The mineral listed as number 10 is the hardest—diamond. Only a diamond can scratch another diamond!

The Mohs' scale does not list every mineral. Instead it lists ten common minerals that have different levels of hardness. Using the Mohs' scale is a simple and useful way to get an idea of how hard a mineral is.

How to Identify a **MINERAL**

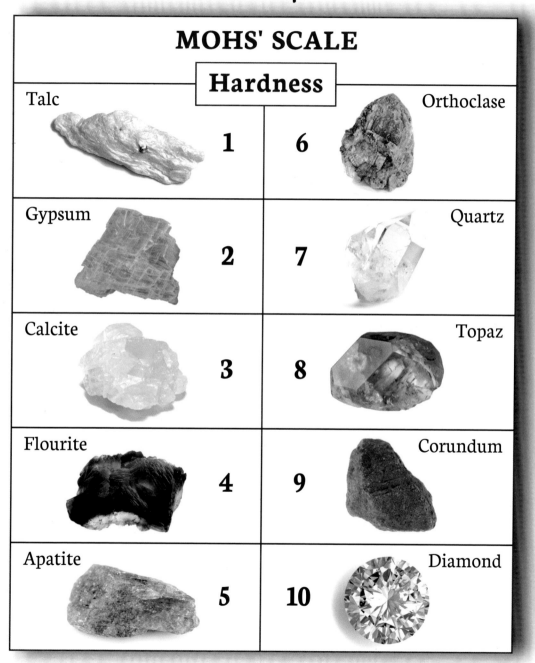

MOHS' SCALE

Hardness

Talc **1**	Orthoclase **6**
Gypsum **2**	Quartz **7**
Calcite **3**	Topaz **8**
Flourite **4**	Corundum **9**
Apatite **5**	Diamond **10**

Luster and Color

Luster is another physical property used to identify minerals. It measures how shiny a mineral is. The mineral graphite is very shiny. It looks metallic when you hold it under a light.

The lead in pencils is a mixture of graphite and clay.

How to Identify a **MINERAL**

Color is another physical property. However, a mineral is not always the same color because of imperfections in the rock. For this reason, color is not the only property scientists use to identify a mineral. They also use the color of a mineral's streak. When you scratch a mineral against a piece of tile, it leaves a streak behind. For example, though the mineral fluorite comes in many colors, such as blue or green, it always leaves a white streak.

Each mineral leaves a different colored streak. Hematite (left) leaves a red streak on the tile. Malachite (right) leaves a green streak.

Did You Know?

There is a birthstone for every month of the year. It is common to have jewelry made from your birthstone.

Birthstones

January		Garnet
February		Amethyst
March		Aquamarine
April		Diamond
May		Emerald
June		Pearl
July		Ruby
August		Peridot
September		Sapphire
October		Opal
November		Topaz
December		Turquoise

How to Identify a **MINERAL**

Taste and Odor

Minerals can also have taste and odor. You should never lick a mineral to see what it tastes like, though, because some are poisonous. There are, however, minerals that are not poisonous and that have a strong taste, such as halite, which is what salt is made from.

Most minerals do not have a strong smell. That can change if the mineral is heated or struck very hard. The mineral barite has no odor until it is heated. Then it smells like rotten eggs!

Barite is a mineral commonly used in textiles, paper, paint, and even makeup.

Fluorescence and Magnetism

Some minerals glow in the dark. This property is called fluorescence. It is named after the mineral fluorite. The other two fluorescent minerals are franklinite and willemite.

Willemite glows under ultraviolet light, which is what the term fluorescent means.

There are a few minerals that are magnetic, which means they draw other metals to them. They are easy to identify. The mineral magnetite is attracted to magnets. A special form of magnetite called lodestone acts like a magnet on its own! It is usually found covered in tiny pieces of metal.

Did You Know?

During the Han dynasty (206 BC–220 AD) the Chinese discovered that one end of a loose stone, called magnetite, always pointed north. Although this discovery was originally used to create order according to the philosophy of *feng shui*, soldiers and sailors later realized they could use it to navigate.

Why Are MINERALS Important?

Minerals make up all the rocks on Earth. Without minerals, there would be no rocks, and the rock cycle would not exist. But minerals are also important to people in different ways. Besides providing people with salt to put on food and graphite to put in pencils, minerals also give people gems and metals.

Beautiful Gemstones

Gems are minerals that have been cut and polished to create beautiful jewels. Diamonds, rubies, sapphires, and emeralds are known as the four most precious gems.

Did You Know?

A lapidary is a worker who cuts and polishes the gemstones that go into jewelry. Lapidaries often cut flat surfaces into the gems, which create facets that reflect light and make the stone sparkle!

Rubies (bottom right) can be red or pink. Rubies, sapphires (left), emeralds (top right), and of course diamonds are very popular—and expensive—gems.

Diamonds are one of the most valuable minerals. For thousands of years, people have worn diamonds as jewelry. They are valued because of their hardness, luster, and beauty. Only 20 percent of the world's diamonds are used to make jewelry. The rest are used to make cutting tools and other machines.

Although rubies are red and sapphires are blue, they are both made from corundum, which is colorless in its pure form. Rubies are created when heat and pressure add bits of mineral called chromium to corundum. Sapphires are produced when the corundum contains the minerals iron and titanium.

Emeralds are made from the mineral beryl. The green color comes from chromium or sometimes vanadium.

Did You Know?

Amethyst is a purple-colored variety of quartz often used in jewelry. It is commonly thought to have healing powers. The largest amethyst mine in North America is in Thunder Bay, Ontario, Canada.

Useful Metals

Some minerals, such as gold and platinum, are metals that occur naturally. Gold can be found in cracks of the Earth's crust called veins, which are often pushed to the surface because of

pressure within the Earth. Pure gold is almost impossible to destroy, but is soft enough to be shaped.

Gold (right), silver, and copper are all found in veins in rocks below the surface of the Earth.

Platinum, found in mines, is one of the heaviest substances on Earth. It is hard and usually used to make jewelry.

Platinum is rare and even more valuable than gold!

Did You Know?

Pyrite, also known as fool's gold, fooled many miners into thinking they had struck it rich.

Sometimes metals combine to form compounds called alloys. Copper and zinc combine to form brass. Tin and copper make the alloy bronze.

Metalworkers often work with minerals. Here, a forge burns coal, another mineral found in the Earth, in order to melt down metals to create alloys.

Why Are MINERALS Important?

Metals are used to build houses, cars, furniture, and many other things. Copper is one of the most useful metals. Copper is good at carrying electricity. Copper wires carry electricity through most homes. Iron, lead, aluminum, and other metals are used to make machines and other tools.

Steel is an alloy made from iron and carbon. It is used to reinforce concrete and large buildings, as well as in major appliances and cars.

Minerals are beautiful to look at and wear, are essential to many industries, and are important in shaping and reshaping Earth's surface as part of the rock cycle.

As long as minerals keep changing to form new rocks, the rock cycle will go on.

Glossary

alloys—Substances composed of two or more elements.

atoms—The smallest parts of elements that can exist either alone or with other elements.

composition—The way something is arranged.

compounds—Two or more things combined.

crystals—In a mineral, crystals are the pattern in which atoms are arranged.

gems—Precious or semiprecious stones that have ornamental value and are usually cut and polished.

igneous rocks—Hot, liquid, underground minerals that have cooled and hardened.

magnetic—Having to do with the force that pulls certain objects toward one another.

minerals—Natural elements that are not animals, plants, or other living things.

properties—Features that belong to something.

sedimentary rocks—Layers of stones, sand, or mud that have been pressed together to form rock.

Further Reading

BOOKS

DK. *Pocket Genius: Rocks and Minerals.* London: DK Publishing, 2012.

Squire, Ann O. *Minerals.* New York: Scholastic, 2012.

Tomacek, Steve. *National Geographic Kids: Dirtmeister's Nitty Gritty Planet Earth: All About Rocks, Minerals, Fossils, Earthquakes, Volcanoes, & Even Dirt!* Washington, DC: National Geographic Kids, 2015.

Zoehfeld, Kathleen Weidner. *National Geographic Readers: Rocks and Minerals.* Washington, DC: National Geographic Children's Books, 2012.

WEBSITES

American Museum of Natural History: Minerals and Gems
amnh.org/our-research/physical-sciences/earth-and-planetary-sciences/collections/minerals-and-gems
See the American Museum of Natural History's collection of minerals and gems.

Science Kids: Rocks and Minerals
sciencekids.co.nz/sciencefacts/earth/rocksandminerals.html
Learn more about naturally occurring minerals in Earth's crust.

Kids Discover: Rocks and Minerals
kidsdiscover.com/spotlight/rocks-and-minerals-for-kids/
A spotlight on rocks and minerals.

Index